LAGRANGE PARK PUBLIC LIBRARY DISTRICT

3 6086 00259 6176

OCT – – 2018

W9-BZP-880

LA GRANGE PARK PUBLIC
LIBRARY DISTRICT
555 N. LA GRANGE RD.
LA GRANGE PARK, IL 60526

FINDING DINOSAURS
ARCHAEOPTERYX

by Rebecca E. Hirsch

FOCUS READERS

WWW.FOCUSREADERS.COM

Copyright © 2018 by Focus Readers, Lake Elmo, MN 55042. All rights reserved. No part of this book may be reproduced or utilized in any form or by any means without written permission from the publisher.

Focus Readers is distributed by North Star Editions:
sales@northstareditions.com | 888-417-0195

Produced for Focus Readers by Red Line Editorial.

Content Consultant: Dr. David B. Weishampel, Professor Emeritus, Center for Functional Anatomy and Evolution, Johns Hopkins University School of Medicine

Photographs ©: Corey Ford/iStockphoto, cover, 1; LadyofHats, 4–5; Paul Fearn/Alamy, 7; Roberto Nistri/Alamy, 9; Uwe Lein/AP Images, 10–11; Red Line Editorial, 12; Qiu Ju Song/Shutterstock Images, 15; World History Archive/Alamy, 17; Pictorum Ikon Images/Newscom, 19; Andreas Meyer/Shutterstock Images, 20–21; paocca/iStockphoto, 23; De Agostini Picture Library Universal Images Group/Newscom, 24; Akkharat Jarusilawong/Shutterstock Images, 26–27; Norbert Michalke/ImageBroker/Alamy, 28

ISBN
978-1-63517-502-8 (hardcover)
978-1-63517-574-5 (paperback)
978-1-63517-718-3 (ebook pdf)
978-1-63517-646-9 (hosted ebook)

Library of Congress Control Number: 2017948059

Printed in the United States of America
Mankato, MN
November, 2017

ABOUT THE AUTHOR

Rebecca E. Hirsch is a PhD-trained scientist and the award-winning author of dozens of books about science for children. She lives in Pennsylvania with her family and assorted pets.

TABLE OF CONTENTS

CHAPTER 1

A SURPRISE IN LIMESTONE

In 1861, workers at a quarry in Germany made a startling discovery. The workers were mining blocks of **limestone**. When they split one block open, they found a fossil of an ancient animal. The animal had four limbs and a long tail. It looked like a small dinosaur. Yet something about the fossil was odd.

Archaeopteryx fossils often include the imprints of feathers or claws.

The workers saw the clear outline of feathers imprinted on the smooth stone. These feathers made it seem like the animal was an ancient bird. But in other ways, the animal was like a dinosaur. For example, it had a bony tail. It had claws on the ends of its front limbs. In contrast, birds have tails made of feathers, not bones. And a bird's front limbs have no claws.

The fossil puzzled many scientists. They were not sure if it was a bird, a dinosaur, or something in between. A German scientist named the animal *Archaeopteryx*. The word is Greek for "ancient wing."

Richard Owen was one of the first scientists to recognize that dinosaurs were different from modern reptiles.

Paleontologist Richard Owen studied this fossil at the Natural History Museum in London, England. The fossil's head was mostly missing, so Owen could not see whether the animal had a birdlike beak.

But he did see the feathers. Owen noticed other birdlike features, too. For instance, the animal had a **furcula**. Birds are the only animals with this bone.

For these reasons, Owen concluded that Archaeopteryx was a bird. Some scientists agreed with him. Others did not. They said Archaeopteryx was both a dinosaur and a bird. They argued that the fossil showed a clear link between dinosaurs and birds. It was evidence that dinosaurs had **evolved** into birds.

For a century after the discovery of Archaeopteryx, most scientists thought it was a bird. But by the 1970s, that belief was changing. Today, scientists say that

The original Archaeopteryx fossil is still on display at the Natural History Museum.

Archaeopteryx was both a bird and a dinosaur. They call Archaeopteryx and other birds "avian" dinosaurs. They call all other dinosaurs "non-avian."

CHAPTER 2

FEATHERED FOSSILS

Scientists have found more than 10 Archaeopteryx fossils in the rocks of southern Germany. These fossils helped them learn what the animal looked like.

The first fossil was discovered in 1861. It was a single feather imprinted on a stone. By 1876, scientists had found a skeleton that included the animal's skull.

A worker unpacks an Archaeopteryx specimen in Munich, Germany.

TIMELINE OF ARCHAEOPTERYX DISCOVERIES

1861

1861
A single feather is discovered. It is given the name *Archaeopteryx lithographica*.

1861
About six weeks later, a partial skeleton with feathers is found.

1876
A more complete skeleton, including a skull, is discovered.

1956
A poorly preserved skeleton with feathers is found in a storage shed in a quarry.

1970
A partial skeleton wrongly identified as a Pterodactylus (originally found in 1855) is correctly identified as Archaeopteryx.

1973
A skeleton wrongly identified as a Compsognathus (originally found in 1951) is correctly identified as Archaeopteryx.

1987
Another Archaeopteryx skeleton is found.

1992
A new Archaeopteryx specimen is found. Because of its heavy breastbone, it is considered a different species, *Archaeopteryx bavarica*.

2005
A partial Archaeopteryx skeleton is discovered.

2011
Another Archaeopteryx skeleton is discovered.

2011

This discovery proved that Archaeopteryx had tiny teeth. These sharp teeth lined the animal's long, narrow snout.

Archaeopteryx skeletons vary in size. The longest one that scientists have found measured 20 inches (50 cm) from snout to tail. But Archaeopteryx was approximately the size of a crow. It probably weighed between 1.8 and 2.2 pounds (0.8 and 1.0 kg).

Archaeopteryx had large eyes. Its neck was thin, similar to the neck of a swan. It had two wide wings. Each wing had three clawed fingers at the tip. The second toe on each foot had a large, curved claw.

Archaeopteryx may have used this claw for stabbing and slashing.

Archaeopteryx was covered with feathers from its head to the tip of its tail. The feathers were not fluffy like the downy feathers on baby birds. Instead, they were flight feathers with

TRANSITIONAL FOSSILS

Archaeopteryx is a transitional fossil. This kind of fossil shows traits of an ancient animal as well as the animal that descended from it. Archaeopteryx shows features of both dinosaurs and birds. Its bones look like the bones of meat-eating dinosaurs called **theropods**. But other features of Archaeopteryx are birdlike, including its feathers.

The flight feathers on a bird's wings are called remiges.

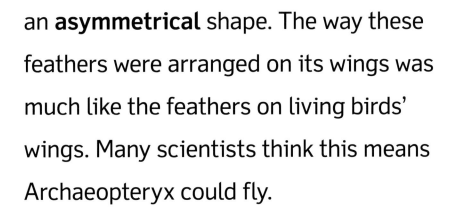

an **asymmetrical** shape. The way these feathers were arranged on its wings was much like the feathers on living birds' wings. Many scientists think this means Archaeopteryx could fly.

Archaeopteryx had many other features needed for flight. For instance, X-rays of its skull revealed that Archaeopteryx had a large brain. This could have helped the animal navigate through the air.

Scientists also compared its bones to the bones of living birds. Like a bird, Archaeopteryx had hollow bones. Hollow bones made the animal's body light enough for flight.

But a living bird has a large breastbone. Its flight muscles attach to this bone. A bird's breastbone has a ridged shape, similar to the pointed front part of a ship. Archaeopteryx's breastbone was smaller and flatter. The way its wings attached to

This model shows what Archaeopteryx may have looked like.

the shoulder meant that it could not move its wings in the way needed for long, slow flight.

After careful study, many scientists concluded that Archaeopteryx was not a strong flier. It may have glided and flapped its wings for short distances. But it probably could not fly very far.

HOW FLIGHT BEGAN

Approximately 160 million years ago, some feathered theropod dinosaurs began to fly. Scientists have proposed two main ideas for how this happened. Some believe flight evolved in animals that lived in trees. Others believe it evolved in fast-running ground animals.

In the "trees-down" hypothesis, flight began when a theropod leapt from branch to branch. As the animal stretched out its wings for balance, it glided. These short glides were the beginnings of flight.

In the "ground-up" hypothesis, the first birds took off from the ground. As a theropod ran after prey, it leapt in short, fluttering hops. The theropod may have even flapped its wings to swat at prey. These short, flapping hops eventually turned into flight.

The first birds, such as Archaeopteryx, may have flown by jumping from trees.

Unfortunately, it is difficult to find evidence to test these hypotheses. However flight began, the bodies of birds gradually changed as they took to the air.

CHAPTER 3

LATE JURASSIC LIFE

Archaeopteryx lived approximately 150 million years ago, during the Late Jurassic period. At this time, dinosaurs dominated life on land. The **supercontinent** Pangaea was splitting into smaller land masses. New oceans flooded the gaps between the land.

Archaeopteryx probably flew short distances.

The area where Archaeopteryx lived is now southern Germany. But at the time, this area was much farther south. The climate was warm and dry, with occasional rainy seasons. During times of rain, seasonal rivers and ponds formed. Most plants in the area were small and bushy. Only a few tall trees grew.

Scientists studied the shape of bones in Archaeopteryx's pelvis, legs, and feet. They concluded that Archaeopteryx probably spent most of its time on the ground, the way chickens do. It walked, ran, and jumped on two legs to chase prey or flee predators. Scientists think it also spent time in trees and bushes. It likely

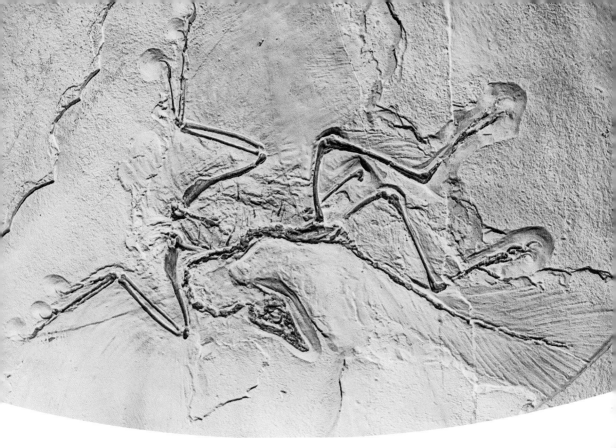

Scientists study fossil specimens to learn about Archaeopteryx's bone structure.

hid, slept, and raised its young in these areas for safety. Some scientists think it jumped or flew, landing on a branch using its clawed feet. Others believe it climbed up off the ground. It might have grasped branches with its claws.

Archaeopteryx may have flown to chase its food.

No **specimen** has been found with its last meal still in its stomach. So, scientists are not sure what Archaeopteryx ate. But they studied the animal's teeth and jaws for clues. Sharp teeth indicate that it ate meat. However, the teeth are small and smooth.

They could not tear meat or crunch through hard bones. Scientists believe Archaeopteryx probably ate insects such as dragonflies and mayflies.

FORMING FOSSILS

Archaeopteryx specimens have been found in limestone at the bottom of a warm, shallow lagoon. Scientists have a theory about how these fossils formed. Strong winds may have blown the animals into the water. This caused the animals to drown. Their bodies sank. They settled in the mud at the bottom of the water. Over many years, the mud built up in layers. Under the weight of the layers, the mud turned to stone. The animal's bones also slowly turned to stone. In some cases, its feathers imprinted in the stone as well.

CHAPTER 4

AN IMPORTANT LINK

Archaeopteryx died out at the end of the Jurassic period. No one knows why it became extinct while other birds survived. Animals often disappear because something about their environment changed. If an animal cannot **adapt** to the new environment, it goes extinct.

Archaeopteryx fossils give scientists important information about the beginning of flight.

Scientists at the Museum of Natural History in Germany study an Archaeopteryx skeleton.

Scientists do not think Archaeopteryx was the direct ancestor of modern birds. It is more like a cousin of living birds. Still, Archaeopteryx has been very important to scientists. It has helped answer questions about the origins of birds. It also provided a clear link between dinosaurs and birds. It gave scientists evidence that some dinosaurs survive and live among us as birds. The Cretaceous period came after the Jurassic ended. During this period, many different kinds of birds evolved. They became widespread around the world. By the Late Cretaceous period, 70 million years after Archaeopteryx, true birds had evolved.

BECOMING BIRDS

Bird fossils from the Cretaceous period have been found on every continent, including Antarctica. Cretaceous birds went through a series of slow changes. Beaks replaced sharp teeth. Long tails became shorter. Breastbones grew larger and changed shape. Over millions of years, they gradually started to look like modern birds.

FOCUS ON
ARCHAEOPTERYX

Write your answers on a separate piece of paper.

1. Write a paragraph describing the world in which Archaeopteryx lived.

2. Do you think Archaeopteryx was more like a bird or a dinosaur? Why?

3. How was Archaeopteryx different from modern birds?

    A. Its flight feathers were arranged differently on its wings.

    B. Its brain was extremely tiny.

    C. Its breastbone was smaller and flatter.

4. How could scientists know for sure what Archaeopteryx ate?

    A. They could find new specimens with food in their stomachs.

    B. They could find a new specimen that included a skull.

    C. They could study the bones of existing specimens.

Answer key on page 32.

GLOSSARY

adapt
To change to better function in a certain place or situation.

asymmetrical
Not able to be divided into two matching halves.

evolved
Changed slowly over time, often becoming more complex.

furcula
The V-shaped bone that is found in front of a bird's breastbone.

limestone
A hard rock that is formed mainly of animal remains, such as shells or coral.

specimen
The remains of an individual animal that show what the entire group of animals was like.

supercontinent
A large continent that existed in the distant past and split apart to produce the present continents.

theropods
A group of meat-eating dinosaurs that had short arms and walked on two legs.

TO LEARN MORE

BOOKS

Alonso, Juan Carlos, and Gregory S. Paul. *The Late Jurassic: Notes, Drawings, and Observations from Prehistory.* Lake Forest, CA: Walter Foster Jr., 2016.

Thimmesh, Catherine. *Scaly Spotted Feathered Frilled: How Do We Know What Dinosaurs Really Looked Like?* Boston: Houghton Mifflin Harcourt, 2013.

Woodward, John. *Dinosaur! Dinosaurs and Other Amazing Prehistoric Creatures as You've Never Seen Them Before.* New York: DK Publishing, 2014.

NOTE TO EDUCATORS

Visit **www.focusreaders.com** to find lesson plans, activities, links, and other resources related to this title.

INDEX

Answer Key: **1.** Answers will vary; **2.** Answers will vary; **3.** C; **4.** A